HOW DO YOU

The Glorious Quran?

HOW DO YOU MEMORISE
The Glorious Quran?

YAHYA GAWTHANI

CLARITAS
BOOKS

1 2 3 4 5 6 7 8 9 10

CLARITAS BOOKS

Bernard Street, Swansea, United Kingdom
Milpitas, California, United States

CLARITAS
BOOKS

First Published in April 2018

Typeset in Minion Pro 14/11

How do you Memorise the Glorious Quran?
By Yahya Gawthani

A CIP catalogue record for this book is available from the British Library

ISBN: 978-1-905837-13-7

بسم الله الرحمن الرحيم

Contents

Foreword

Praise be to Allah who is responsible for the preservation of His Book and has prepared in every age a group of people who are committed to its preservation, guarding every letter, even in their inflexion. May the peace and blessings of Allah be upon the leader of the reciters in this world and in the Hereafter, our Prophet Muhammad, possessor of outstanding qualities, and upon his family and his companions.

To proceed, I have read the excellent and unique treatise entitled *How Do You Memorise the Glorious Quran*? written by the beloved brother and scholar – Yahya Gawthani, may Allah protect him. I have seen that the treatise mentions well-known methods of memorising the Quran, but it also includes modern ones. There is no doubt that diversity in the methods of memorising the Quran eliminates boredom.

Many people have stopped me to ask about the best way to memorise the Quran. Then along came the treatise of Shaykh Yayha, may Allah protect him, with the sufficient answer and the pure spring for those wanting to memorise the Quran – both children and adults.

I ask Allah to make this book beneficial to all those who read it and to bless the author and increase his usefulness especially for the people of the Quran and Muslims in general. Verily, He is able to do so.

May the peace and blessings of Allah be upon our leader and prophet Muhammad, upon his family and his companions. All

Praise is due to Allah.

Shaykh Ayman Rushdi Swayd
Servant of the Glorious Quran
Jeddah
1/6/1414

Chapter 1

The Quran and Why to Memorise It

THE PRESERVATION OF THE QURAN

Muslims believe that the Quran has been preserved in its original form and that Allah the Exalted has protected the Quran from any modification or fabrication.

Preservation of the Quran in the Preserved Tablet *(al-lawh al-mahfudh)*

This is truly a glorious Quran [written] on a preserved Tablet.[1]

The word "preserved" (*mahfudh*) appears in the Arabic in the genitive case (the last letter has a *kasra*), indicating that it is an adjective modifying the word "tablet" (*lawh*). This indicates that whatever is written or contained in the tablet is preserved. There is also another reading of the word "tablet", in which it appears in the nominative case (the last letter has a *damma*): in this case, it is an adjective modifying the word "Quran", indicating that the Quran is preserved in the Tablet.

It is truly exalted in the Source of Scripture kept with Us, and full of wisdom.[2]

Preservation of the Quran by Revealing it to Prophet Muhammad ﷺ

He is the One who knows what is hidden. He does not disclose it except to a messenger of His choosing. He sends watchers to go in front and behind.[3]

This shows that when the angel Jibril brought the revelation of the Quran, there were angels with him protecting the revelation and surrounding the Prophet ﷺ as the Quran was being revealed to him, as stated on the authority of Sa'd ibn Jabir and Dahhak.[4]

We tried to reach heaven, but discovered it to be full of stern guards and shooting stars.[5]

The Quran was protected in the heavens by "stern guards" (i.e., angels), so that not even a letter from the Quran was stolen, and as for those who made an attempt (to tamper with the words of Allah), flaming fires were awaiting them.

We used to sit in places there, listening, but anyone trying to listen now will find a shooting star lying in wait for him.[6]

This refers to the situation before the sending of the Prophet Muhammad ﷺ and before the beginning of the revelation of the Quran.

Preservation of the Quran in the Heart of Prophet Muhammad ﷺ

[Prophet], do not rush your tongue in an attempt to hasten [your memorisation of] the Revelation: We shall make sure of its safe collection and recitation. When We have recited it, repeat the recitation and We shall make it clear.[7]

It is narrated in Bukhari on the authority of Ibn Abbas, referring to the saying of Allah mentioned above, that the Prophet Muhammad ﷺ would be affected physically (i.e., moving his tongue and lips) when receiving revelation.[8]

Allah also says:

> The disbelievers also say, "Why was the Quran not sent down to him all at once?" We sent it in this way to strengthen your heart [Prophet]; We gave it to you in gradual revelation.[9]

Thus, the Quran has been preserved by Allah in the heart of the Prophet Muhammad ﷺ.

Preservation of the Quran by its Recitation by the Prophet Muhammad ﷺ

Allah says:

> We have caused Our Word to come to them so that they may be mindful.[10]

Allah also says:

> Messenger, proclaim everything that has been sent down to you from your Lord – if you do not, then you will not have communicated His message – and God will protect you from people. God does not guide those who defy Him.[11]

He also says:

> He does not speak from his own desire. The Quran is nothing less than a revelation that is sent to him.[12]

He also says:

> Just as We have sent among you a Messenger of your own to recite Our revelations to you, purify you and teach you the Scripture, wisdom, and [other] things you did not know.[13]

The above Quranic texts are conclusive evidence that the Prophet Muhammad ﷺ preached the Quran (both its recitation and its teachings) as it was revealed to him; he neither added a single letter nor did he delete a single letter.

Preservation of the Quran by Allah Until the Day of Judgement

Allah says:

> We have sent down the Quran Ourself, and We Ourself will guard it. Even before you [Prophet].[14]

This preservation necessitates three things:

First, it necessitates preservation of its letters and words, as they were revealed to Prophet Muhammad ﷺ.

Second, it necessitates the explanation of the Quran through the hadith.

Third, it necessitates the preservation of the *dawah* (propagation) of the Quran, meaning that Allah chose certain servants to memorise the Quran and recite it.

THE VIRTUES OF MEMORISING THE QURAN

Allah says:

> We have made it easy to learn lessons from the Quran: will anyonetakeheed?[15]

The Quran has been made easy to understand and easy to memorise. Imam al-Qurtubi said: "The verse means: 'We have made it easy for memorisation and will help those who intend to memorise it; is there any student [prepared] to memorise the Quran so that We may help them?' "[16]

Allah also says:

> But no, [this Quran] is a revelation that is clear to the hearts of those endowed with knowledge. No one refuses

to acknowledge Our revelations but the evildoers.[17]

This verse exclaims the greatness of those hearts which memorise the Word of Allah and describes the people possessing such hearts as people of knowledge. Truly, there is no knowledge after the Book of Allah. It also makes clear that Allah selects from his servants a group whose hearts are made as vessels (i.e., to be filled with the Quran).

What is surprising is that from amongst this group of people are those who do not speak Arabic, yet they are able to recite the Quran fluently and memorise it.

Memorisation of the Quran in the Eyes of the Prophet Muhammad ﷺ

It has been established that the Prophet ﷺ gave preference to those amongst his companions who had memorised the Quran. When a delegation was sent by the Prophet ﷺ, he would often say: "The leader amongst you [should] be the one who [has] the most knowledge of the Quran."[18] After the battles, when the martyrs amongst the Companions were gathered, the one with the most knowledge (in terms of memorisation) of the Quran would be buried first, and the Prophet ﷺ himself would gave the martyr glad tidings.[19] In certain cases, the amount of Quran that a man had memorised would serve as the *mahr* (dowry) to be given to the woman he intended to marry.[20] The flag of war in battles would also be given to the one who had memorised the most Quran.

Abdullah ibn Amr ibn al-Aas ؓ narrated that the Prophet ﷺ said: "It will said to the companion of the Quran (on the Day of Judgement): 'Read and recite as you used to recite in the world; verily, your station is at the last verse you read.' "[21]

Walid ibn Muslim said: "When we used to sit (in the circles of) al-Awza'i, he used to see someone amongst us talking. He would say: 'O boy, have you read the Quran?' If he (the boy) replied: 'yes', he would say: 'Read [from such and such a verse].' If he replied 'no', he would say 'go from here and learn the Quran before you seek knowledge.'"[22]

THE OBLIGATION OF REVISING THE QURAN

Allah created the human being forgetful. Forgetfulness has many causes, including the lack of revision and an abundance of work. Several hadiths have been narrated by the Companions warning against forgetting what one has memorised of the Quran. It is sufficient to mention the following.

Abu Musa al-Ash'ari ﵁ narrated that the Prophet ﷺ said: "Make this Quran a contract. By the One in Whose Hands is myself, it slips away faster than a camel from its cord."[23]

Ibn Umar ﵁ narrated that the Prophet ﷺ said: "Verily, the example of the companion of the Quran is like the example of the corded camel (tied with a knot): if one binds it, they have caught it; if they set it loose, it will go."[24]

Anas ibn Malik ﵁ narrated that the Prophet ﷺ said: "I was shown the rewards of my *ummah* (nation) to the point that I saw a harmful thing that someone removes form the mosque. And I was [also] shown the sins of my *ummah*, and I did not see a sin greater than a surah or an ayah from the Quran that was given to a person [i.e., they memorised it] and then he or she forgot it."[25]

Sa'd ibn Ubadah ﵁ narrated that the Prophet ﷺ said: "The one who reads the Quran and then forgets it will meet Allah on the Day of Judgement mutilated"[26]

Allah says:

> In this way We relate to you [Prophet] stories of what happened before. We have given you a Quran from Us. Whoever turns away from it will bear on the Day of Resurrection a heavy burden.[27]

He also says:

> But whoever turns away from it will have a life of great hardship. We shall bring him blind to the Assembly on the Day of Resurrection, and he will say, "Lord, why did You bring me here blind? I was sighted before!" God will say, "This is how it is: You ignored Our revelations when they came to you, so today you will be ignored."[28]

The apparent meaning of these verses refers to the reading and reciting of the Quran, even though most of the commentators understood it to refer to the forgetfulness in acting by the Quran.

Ibn Kathir said: "Some of the commentators on the Quran have interpreted the verse as referring to the one who avoids the recitation of the Quran and is exposed to forgetfulness and his lack of attaching importance to it."[29]

It is narrated that Dahhak ibn Mazahim said: "There is no one who learns the Quran then forgets it except that they will commit a sin, because Allah says, 'Whatever misfortune befalls you [people], it is because of what your own hands have done.'[30] And verily forgetting the Quran is amongst the greatest trials and difficulties."[31]

Allah says:

> And during the night wake up and pray, as an extra offering of your own, so that your Lord may raise you to a [highly] praisedstatus.[32]

THE CONDITIONS FOR SEEKING KNOWLEDGE

Imam Shafi'i ﵀ said: "Do not acquire knowledge except with six [things]. I will inform you of their explanation with clarification: intelligence, aspiration, effort, competency, accompanying a teacher and a long time."[33]

Intelligence

Intelligence is of two kinds: one is given as a gift from Allah, and the other is acquired. Both are from Allah, but in your capacity as a human being, you can develop the second kind of intelligence, especially during childhood.

In Japan, children enter primary school at the age of three and are taught by competent teachers, who develop the children's skills and talents. The children complete their secondary education at the age of fourteen, but they surpass the graduates of our universities in terms of their general knowledge and academic culture.

Aspiration

Students of knowledge should aspire to reach their goals and should regard their learning as a trust.

Effort

Students should exert their utmost effort in reaching their aims. This should include determination and daily revision.

Competency

Even with high aspirations and significant effort, no one can reach their goal without competency.

A Teacher

Seeking knowledge and learning the Quran is not possible without the guidance of a teacher. When one studies any discipline, and especially the Quran, one should do so under the guidance of a teacher, so that the knowledge is acquired in its rightful manner and so that any ambiguities in the meanings have been made clear. It is for this reason that scholars say that "the one who took their books as a teacher will have a wrong understanding that will overweigh their correct understanding."

Time

Many students study and attend the circles of a teacher determined to seek knowledge, but they continue their studies for only a short period of time. What is even worse is that upon their completion of their short study, they believe they have acquired knowledge and that by memorising a few issues of *fiqh* (jurisprudence), they are now in the position to issue fatwas, present their own *ijtihad* (arriving at a ruling using independent reason), and rebut the opinions of the great scholars – for the door of *ijtihad* is open for all!

Both of these situations are very dangerous. Seeking knowledge is not merely attending lessons for a few months; it requires a long period of time accompanying the scholars.

Abdullah ibn al-Mubarak said: "Do not seek knowledge except with time, money, memorisation and *taqwa* (God-consciousness)."[34]

Chapter 2

Basic Principles and Rules

In this chapter I will discuss the most important principles that need to be understood and implemented by the one intending to memorise the Quran.

FIRST PRINCIPLE – SINCERITY AND *Tawfiq* (SUCCESS)

Sincerity of intention (*ikhlas*) and memorising only to seek the pleasure of Allah are vital elements in order to acquire the help of Allah in memorising the Quran. Allah says:

> Say: "I have been commanded to serve God, dedicating my worship entirely to Him."[35]

As for the one who memorises the Quran in order to be singled out as a person who has memorised the Quran, there is no reward for them. The Prophet ﷺ said: "The first people who will be judged on the Day of Judgement are three." He mentioned from amongst them a person who acquired knowledge and taught it and also learnt the Quran. "They will be asked as to what they had done with it. They will reply: 'I acquired knowledge and taught it and I learnt the Quran.' It will be said to them: 'You have lied; you learnt the Quran so that people will call you *qari* (reciter).' They will then be dragged on their face and thrown into the fire."[36]

Ali ibn al-Madani said: "When I bid Sufyan farewell, he said to me, 'Verily you will be tested in this matter and the people will be in need of you, so fear Allah and purify your intention.' "[37]

The Prophet ﷺ said: "Verily actions are judged by intentions."[38]

When a student memorises the Quran seeking only the pleasure of Allah, they will feel a sense of great pleasure and happiness, and this feeling will help them overcome the many obstacles in the memorisation of the Quran.

SECOND PRINCIPLE – MEMORISING IN YOUTH IS LIKE ENGRAVING ON STONE

The mind of a child is clearer than the mind of an adult. Hence, memorisation at a young age is a vital aid in memorising the Quran. It has been narrated that the Prophet ﷺ said: "The memorisation of a child is comparable to engraving on a stone; the memorisation of an adult, once they have grown older, is comparable to writing on water."[39]

Ibn Majah relates that the Prophet ﷺ said: "The one who read the Quran before attaining puberty is amongst those who have been given judgement in their youth."[40]

Those who learn the Quran during their childhood merge the Quran with their blood and body because that is the period when the mind and body develop and grow. Imam Bukhari narrates in his *al-Tarikh al-Kabir* that the Prophet ﷺ said: "The one who learns the Quran in their youth, Allah merges it [the Quran] with their meat and blood [i.e., they do not forget it]."[41]

The most suitable age to begin memorising the Quran is at the age of five or even at a younger age with the help of Quranic recitations on audio. Children can memorise what they listen to with concentration very easily.

If while reading this, you begin to regret that your own days of memorising the Quran have passed and that you did not memorise the Quran in your childhood, then do not regret. Verily, the one who has a strong determination to memorise the Quran will be able to memorise it if they put that aim before their eyes.

However, I do not know of anyone who has memorised the entire Quran after the age of forty.

THIRD PRINCIPLE – CHOOSING THE RIGHT TIME

It has been established from the experiences of many that the best times for memorisation are at dawn and after Fajr, for these are times at which the mind is clear and the body is at rest.

Al-Khatib al-Baghdadi said: "Know that for memorisation are certain hours. It is obligatory for the one who wants to memorise to abide by them. The best of times is dawn." And it was asked of some of the scholars, "With what have you acquired knowledge?" One said, "with the light and sitting till the morning". Another said, "with traveling [to seek knowledge] and sitting vigil at night and at dawn".[42]

It has been narrated that Ismail ibn Abu Uways said, "If you want to memorise something, then sleep and wake up at dawn, put the light on, and look [at the piece to be memorised]. Surely you will not forget it after that, Allah willing."[43]

Late at night is also a suitable time to memorise, for the heart is free from any worries or anxieties. Thus, when Hammad ibn Zayd was asked: "What is the most helpful of things in memorisation?" he replied, "a lack of worry and anxiety".[44]

FOURTH PRINCIPLE – CHOOSING THE RIGHT PLACE

The choice of a place to memorise has a practical effect on memorisation, and it is preferred that the place does not contain many objects, drawings, or other distracting things. Some scholars prefer a surrounding full of trees and gardens; I myself have experimented with this and have found it beneficial.

Al-Khatib al-Baghdadi said: "Know that for memorisation there are (certain suitable) places for the one who intends to memorise."[45]

The place should be free from any external noises (such as children playing or cars). Memorisation requires one to be in a peaceful and undisturbed surrounding.

A mosque can be a suitable place for memorisation, depending on the time. Many have the habit of walking and memorising, for this helps to consolidate that which has been memorised.

FIFTH PRINCIPLE – RECITING WITH *Tajwid* AND A MELODIOUS TONE

The Quran has many characteristics. Of these are three things which distinguish it phonetically from everyday Arabic.

Firstly, Quran has an increase in the length of *ghunnah* (nasalisation) in the letters *nun* and *mim* (when they have a *shaddah*), in *idgham* (merging of the letters), and *ikhfa* (concealing the sound of certain letters).

Secondly, it has an increase in the length of *madd* (prolongation of sound) in certain places.

Thirdly, there is the melodious tone in which the Quran is recited.

The Quran should not only be recited in a melodious tone but also with *tajwid* (rules which are to be applied whilst reciting the Quran). Both of these help in the memorisation of the Quran. The Prophet ﷺ said: "The one who does not sing the Quran is not from amongst us."[46] He also said in another narration: "Improve [the recitation] of the Quran with your voices; verily, a nice voice increases the beauty and excellence of the Quran."[47]

It is better to develop and recite the Quran in your own style of recitation rather than to imitate others. You should also make sure that whilst you are reciting the Quran in order to memorise it, you recite in an audible voice (i.e., so that the recitation can be heard by yourself and others).

Zubayr ibn Bakkar said: "My father came to me and found me reflecting in my notebook and not reading in a voice that was audible. He said to me: 'For you is your narration [hadith] which your eyes will take to your heart. If you want [to memorise] the narration, look at it and pronounce it so that it is audible. Then your eyes will take it to your heart, and your listening will convey it to your heart.' "[48]

Abu Hilal al-Askari said: "It is obligatory for the one who studies to raise their voice so that they can hear themselves. Whatever the ear is made to listen to is deeply rooted in the heart."

SIXTH PRINCIPLE – TO USE ONLY ONE QURAN

It is highly recommended that the one intending to memorise the Quran memorise and revise from only one published version of the Quran rather than memorising from many different prints of the Quran. From amongst the best printed versions of the Quran is the *Mushaf al-Huffadh*, published by King Fahd in Medina.[49] Restricting oneself to a specific print consolidates the memorisation and prevents confusion whilst memorising the verses of a page.

SEVENTH PRINCIPLE – ACCURACY OVER QUANTITY

Before beginning the memorisation of any part of the Quran, you should first make sure that you recite it correctly with *tajwid*. This is not possible for an individual alone. A qualified teacher must listen to your recitation; for the Quran is taken from the teacher, who takes it from their teachers, and so on, until the *sanad* (chain of transmission) reaches back to the Prophet ﷺ. If it is not possible to read to a qualified teacher, then audio recitations by qualified readers of the Quran should be used.

The experiences of many have proven that those who begin memorising the Quran before they have corrected their recitation will find it difficult to free themselves of their mistakes, even if they realise they are making mistakes. Those who correct their recitation before memorising the Quran will complete its memorisation before those who memorise without rectifying their recitation.

EIGHTH PRINCIPLE – VISUALLY CONNECTING THE VERSES

One of the most important principles of memorisation is to visually and mentally connect the beginnings and endings of verses. You can do this by reading the end of a verse, and then quickly, without stopping, joining it to the beginning of the next verse.

Repeat this practice at least five times between the end of a verse and the beginning of the next, between the end of a *juz* and the beginning of the next, and between the end of a surah and the beginning of the next. This will solve the problem of forgetfulness during recitation, which is a problem the majority of Quran students face.

It is also very beneficial to connect between the ending of a page and the beginning of another; this can be practiced by trying to remember the beginnings and endings of all of the pages of a certain *juz*, for example, before going to sleep.

In addition to this, you should memorise the beginnings of the quarters. (Every *juz* has two *hizb*, and every *hizb* has four quarters. Therefore, every *juz* is made up of eight quarters.). Concentrate on the first word of every quarter.

Let us take the first *juz* as an example.

First *Hizb*
First quarter: الحمد لله رب العالمين
Second quarter: إن الله لا يستحي أن
Third quarter: أتأمرون الناس بالبر
Fourth quarter: وٌإزا سنسقى موسى

Second *Hizb*
First quarter: أ فتطمعون أن يؤمنوا
Second quarter:ولقد جاءكم موسى
Third quarter: ما نسخ من اية
Fourth quarter: وإزا بتلي إبراهيم

Applying this method to all of the chapters of the Quran will not take more than a few minutes, but it will help consolidate your memorisation.

NINTH PRINCIPLE – CONTINUOUS REPETITION

Students differ in their capacity to memorise; some are able to memorise with little or no repetition whilst others cannot memorise except with continuous repetition.

Repetition is of two kinds: silent and loud.

Silent repetition is done when students scan or quickly revise verses without verbally pronouncing the words.

Sufyan al-Thawri said: "Make the hadith your own speech and the thoughts of your heart. Then you will [be able to] memorise it."[50]

In the same way, it can be said that if you "make the Quran your own speech and the thoughts of your heart, you will be able to memorise it".

Al-Izz ibn Abdul Salam said: "I have not slept a night except that I have revised a chapter of *fiqh* in my heart before sleeping."[51]

During loud repetition, students raise their voices. It is absolutely necessary for those who want to memorise well that they continuously repeat the verses aloud. They should repeat the verses many times and not suffice by repeating them once or twice.

Ibn al-Jawzi said: "Al-Hasan ibn Abu Bakr al-Naysaburi said to us: 'I cannot memorise a lesson until I repeat it fifty times.' "

Abu Ishaq al-Shayrazi used to repeat his lessons one hundred times.[52]

A lot of repetition and revision can be tiring, but the results in the long term are worth the effort. Those who do not repeat the verses they have memorised a sufficient number of times will forget what they have memorised.

Ibn al-Jawzi said: "Al-Hasan told us that a student of knowledge was continuously repeating his lessons in his house, and an old woman in his house said to him: 'By Allah! I have already memorised it!' He said to her: 'Repeat it.' She repeated it. After a few days he said to the woman: 'Repeat that lesson.' She said: 'I have not memorised it.' He said: 'I repeat that which I memorise so that I am not afflicted with what has afflicted you [i.e., forgetfulness].'"[53]

TENTH PRINCIPLE – CONSISTENT DAILY REVISION

In the early stages, committing the *nafs* (the self) to anything is a difficult task. The *nafs*, by its nature, is not inclined to commit itself to the task of memorisation. Many students avoid subjects that demand a lot of memorisation. However, if the *nafs* is able to commit itself to memorisation, the memorisation will become something beloved to the *nafs*.

One of the important principles in the memorisation of the Quran is to commit yourself to daily memorisation and to select a certain amount (of verses) to be memorised. If you abide by that amount daily and avoid the whispers of Shaytan and laziness, you will find that the task of memorising the Quran has become as integral a part of your daily life as eating and drinking.

Al-Zuhri said: "Verily a man does not seek [knowledge and memorisation] except that his heart [is like] a mountain path from among many mountain paths. Then it does not take long before it becomes a valley, and nothing is put in it except that it is swallowed."[54] Meaning that, when someone begins to seek knowledge, their memory will be very narrow, but after a short while, they will not have difficulty retaining information and will become accustomed to memorisation. Their hearts will swallow the knowledge as the valley swallows up everything.

Abu al-Samh al-Ta'i said: "I used to listen to my uncle in his circles reciting poetry, and if I joined them, they insulted me and scolded me, saying, 'Do you listen to something and do not memorise it?' " He said: "Memorisation was difficult for me but when I began to desire and crave it, I became accustomed to it to the extent that I memorised the *qaseedah* (a long poem) of Ru'bah and the *qaseedah* of Qatim al-A'maq in one night, although they had approximately two hundred verses each."[55]

You must devote a certain part of your day, regardless of how long or short it may be, to memorisation; for continuous drops of water on a rock will result in a hole.

Abu Hilal al-Askari said: "Ahmad ibn al-Furat did not let a day pass without memorising something, even if it was very little." And others said: "I used to attend the circles of the shaykh early in the morning on Friday when there wasn't a lesson, so that I do not break my habit of attending [the circles]."[56]

Another important aspect of memorisation is to give yourself a day or two of rest each week and not memorise during these days. This will help in firmly establishing the memorisation in your memory.

Ibn al-Jawzi said: "Students should rest themselves from memorisation a day or two weekly, so that it becomes like a building that is given a rest in order to become stable."[57]

You should also select a specific *juz* to be memorised in a specific time. Once you have memorised it, give yourself a rest for a few days and then return again to the memorisation.

Al-Khatib al-Baghdadi said: "Students should set themselves a limit. Every time they reach it, they should stop memorising for a few days, as is the case in the building of a house. Do you not see that the one who intends to build a solid house builds a few cubits, then leaves it to stabilise, then builds on top of it? If it was built in one day, it would not be a stable building, and it may collapse quickly. In the same way, students must set goals. Every time they reach these goals, they should stop so that what is already in their hearts stabilises."[58]

It is also very important that you do not memorise in times of anxiety and grief. If you ever find yourself in such a state, leave the memorisation, and take a rest or occupy yourself with things that do not demand complete concentration and attention of your mind (i.e., reading stories or even poetry, for there is a benefit in that).[59]

ELEVENTH PRINCIPLE – SLOW, CALM MEMORISATION

The role that the lens of the eyes plays in memorisation is a very important one and can be compared to the role of the lens of a camera. The photographer moves the camera and positions it slowly and attentively toward the object that needs to be photographed and then, with precision, takes a photograph.

In the same way, if you want to memorise a page from the Quran, it is necessary for you to read the verses slowly and then repeat them continuously so that you master them. The slower and calmer the memorisation, the better the material will be retained in the memory. Whereas, if the memorisation is completed rapidly and in a hurry, you will only memorise words from here and lines from there and your memorisation will be shaky. You will need to memorise it again as though you had not memorised it before.

This was clearly observed in our circles of memorisation. Students assigned a page to memorise would return after a few minutes claiming that they had memorised it, and most probably, they had memorised it with a few mistakes. However, it is the duty of the teacher to pay attention to the time which students spend memorising and not to accept rapid memorisation.

We have learnt from experience, that the verses that students memorise with calmness and extreme concentration and repetition will be more firmly established in the memory than other verses. It is for this reason that some of those who have memorised the Quran know some surahs better than others (i.e., they exerted a more concentrated effort in the memorisation of some surahs than others).

Al-Khatib al-Baghdadi said: “It is necessary for students to memorise carefully, not doing a lot but only a little, according to what they can retain, and to try to understand its meaning.” Allah says:

The disbelievers also say, "Why was the Quran not sent down to him all at once?" We sent it in this way to strengthen your heart [Prophet]; We gave it to you in gradual revelation.[60]

TWELFTH PRINCIPLE - CONCENTRATING ON VERSES THAT ARE SIMILAR PREVENTS CONFUSION

From amongst the obstacles many students face during their memorisation is the problem of the similarity of certain verses with others. For example,

فاصبحو في ديرهم[62] and فاصبحوا في دارهم[61]

Students may hesitate or make a mistake when they reach these two verses.

There are many ways to overcome these similar verses. Many of the commentators of the Quran have pointed out these methods. The best way for you to overcome this obstacle is for you to be guided by your teacher when you come across such verses. For example, when you are reading Surah al-Baqarah, and you reach the verse where Allah says:

و يقتلون النبيين بغير الحق[63] (1)

Your teacher should remind you that this verse appears in the Quran three times. The first is here in al-Baqarah, and the other two times are in Surah Ali Imran:

و يقتلون النبيين بغير حق[64] (2)

يقتلون الأنبياء بغير حق[65] (3)

Your teacher should ask you to record these verses in your notebook. When you reach any of these verses during your revision, remind yourself of the other verses in the other places. Also, if you hear someone else reciting any of these verses, guide them as your teacher guided you. Hence, the role of the teacher is of absolute importance. (I will elaborate on this role in the principle that follows.)

There are also many books that deal with this subject:

Some include analysis, such as *Fath al-Rahman* by Shaykh al-Islam Zakariyya al-Ansari and *Mutashabih al-Quran* by Abul-Hasan al-Munadi. Some do not include analysis, such as *Sabeel al-Tasbeet wal-Yaqeen li Huffadh* by Abdul Hameed Saffi al-Deen, *Tanbeeh al-Hafi Ila Ayat al-Mutashabihat al-Alfadh* by Muhammad Abdul Aziz al-Musnad, *Dhabtul Mutashabihat fil Quran al-Karim* by Muhammad ibn Abdullah al-Sageer and *Awn al-Rahman fi Hifdh al-Quran* by al-Qamouni. Others approach the subject in the form of poetry, such as *Nazm al-Mutashabihat al-Quran* by Muhammad al-Tasheti, *Manzumat al-Deemiyati* and *Manzumat al-Sakhawi*.

THIRTEENTH PRINCIPLE – THE IMPORTANCE OF MEMORISING UNDER THE GUIDANCE OF A TEACHER

Attaching oneself to a teacher is of vital importance, for the Quran is learnt by taking it from a teacher and not just the mere reading of it.

In the beginning stages of your memorisation, a teacher can help you solve the problems that you face and guide you in your memorisation of the Quran. They should remind you constantly to seek refuge from Allah and to seek His pleasure only.

Al-Qabasi said: "It has always been [the tradition of] the Muslims to teach their children the Quran by bringing them to teachers."[66]

"The need of a student for a teacher to pass along to them what they know is as great a need as the need for a teacher who will clarify the thoughts of youth, awaken their feelings, give life to their intellect, improve their understanding and arm them with the truth in the face of falsehood, virtues to kill vices and knowledge to destroy ignorance."[67]

Sitting in the circles can have a great effect on the purification and development of the *nafs* (the self). Luqman al-Hakim said to his son: "What have you benefitted from your wisdom?" He said: "I do not take that which does not help or benefit me." He said: "O my son! Sit with the scholars [so much so that] you press them with your knees. Verily, Allah revives the dead hearts with wisdom as He gives life to the dead earth by the showers of the sky."[68]

How should you choose a teacher?

There are certain principles to keep in mind while choosing a teacher.

1. SEARCH, LOOK AND PONDER

You must search for a teacher who fulfils all the criteria, and you should not be hasty but should do so after thinking a lot about it and reflecting on it. Al-Zarnuji said: "And we chose Abu Hanifah Hammad ibn Salma after a great deal of reflection."[69]

Al-Zarnuji also said: "Hakim guided some of the students of knowledge: 'If you go to Bukhra, then do not hasten in leaving the scholars. Stay for two months so that you can ponder and choose a teacher; for if you went to a scholar and started your lessons with them, their lessons may not appeal to you. Leave them and go to another as there will be no *barakah* (blessing) in it. Then reflect for two months before choosing a teacher.' "[70]

2. TAKE THE ADVICE OF RELIABLE AUTHORITIES

Ask those who are specialised in the sciences of the Quran and *tajwid* (rules which are to be applied whilst reciting the Quran), for this is a general Islamic principle: "[Those who] conduct their affairs by mutual consultation".[71]

It is also said: "The one who consults is saved from humiliation."[72]

3. PRAY *ISTIKHARAH*

Ibn Jama'ah said: "It is necessary for students to contemplate and ask Allah for guidance in choosing a teacher from whom they will take knowledge, observe good character, and learn *adab* (manners)."[73]

Requirements which the teacher must meet

There are many requirements and conditions that the teacher should meet and fulfil. From amongst these requirements are the following.

1. CORRECT *AQIDAH*

The *aqidah* (creed) of the teacher should be in accordance with the *aqidah* of *Ahl al-Sunnah wal-Jama'ah*. As some of the pious predecessors said: "This knowledge is the deen (religion). So look at the one from who you take your deen."[74]

2. ABUNDANT KNOWLEDGE

The teacher should possess knowledge of the Quran and have *taqwa* (God-consciousness).

3. ABILITY TO TEACH OTHERS

Ibn Jama'ah says as a summary of the important characteristics that a teacher should possess: "They should be from amongst those who have perfected their competency and those who have been proven to be compassionate, whose virtue and modesty is well known, whose respect is wide spread and are the best in teaching and the best in helping others understand."[75]

4. *HIFDH* OF THE QURAN AND PERFECT RECITATION

The teacher should be known amongst the people of knowledge and preferably have a *sanad* (chain going back to the Prophet) and know the ten *qira'at* (ways of reciting the Quran). If you cannot find a teacher who fulfils these conditions, then choose a teacher who you think will be suitable to teach you. If you cannot find a teacher at all, then ask the help of a brother or sister. The student who recites the Quran on their own and just reads to themselves will not be able to recognise their own mistakes.

FOURTEENTH PRINCIPLE – LOOK AT AND WRITE THE VERSES

Looking at the page you are memorising is one of the basic tools needed in the memorisation of the Quran. You should be able to picture the page in your mind; this will help in retaining and consolidating the memorisation in a systematic manner.

It has been narrated that Abu Masud Ahmad ibn al-Furat said: "We still hear our teachers mentioning things related to memorisation, and they agreed that there is nothing more intense or lasting than looking [at the page or verses to be memorised]."[76]

Many of our scholars, may Allah be pleased with them all, have pointed out the importance of looking with concentration at the verses to be memorised.

Ismail ibn Abu Uways said in reply to a question: "If you intend to memorise something, sleep and then wake up at dawn and light [the lamp]. Then look at it and you will not forget it afterwards, if Allah wills."[77]

FIFTEENTH PRINCIPLE – ENJOIN THE GOOD AND REFRAINING FROM EVIL

Enjoining acts of obedience and doing righteous deeds gives light and *sakinah* (tranquillity) to the heart, which leads to clarity of the mind, which leads to easy memorisation. In contrast, the heart which has committed acts of disobedience is darkened. Hence, Allah takes away the blessing of knowledge and memorisation from the one who disobeys Him.

It has been narrated that Abdullah ibn Masud said: "I charge the one who forgets knowledge that they used to know, of wrongful deeds that they have committed."[78]

Sufyan ibn Uyaynah was once asked: "Is knowledge taken away from a person because of the sins they commit?" He replied:

> Have you not heard the saying of Allah: "But they broke their pledge, so We distanced them [from Us] and hardened their hearts. They distort the meaning of [revealed] words and have forgotten some of what they were told to remember: you [Prophet] will always find treachery in all but a few of them."[79] And that was the Book of Allah, the greatest knowledge and the greatest blessing with which they were favoured and which (later) became a witness against them.[80]

Imam Malik ﵀ was once asked: "Is there anything that is beneficial to memorisation?" He replied: "If there was such a thing, it would be the leaving of wrongful and sinful deeds."[81]

Ali ibn Khasram said to Waki' ibn al-Jarrah: "I am a stupid man, and memorisation is not easy for me. Teach me a cure for difficulty in memorisation." Waki' said: "O My son! I have not tried any cure for memorisation except that of refraining from wrongful and sinful deeds."[82]

This is the advice given to us by our righteous predecessors ﵃. It may also be appropriate to cite the saying of Imam al-Shafi'i: "I complained to Waki' about my bad memorisation. He guided me towards the leaving of sinful deeds and informed me that knowledge is a light. And the light of Allah does not guide a sinner."

Knowledge must be combined with action. Allah says:

> It is most hateful to God that you say things and then do not do them.[83]

Sufyan al-Thawri said: "Knowledge calls out to action. It responds to it or leaves it."[84]

Imam al-Ghazali said: "If you acquired knowledge for a hundred years and collected thousands of books, you still would not be prepared for the mercy of Allah except with action."[85]

Allah says:

And that man will only have what he has worked towards.[86]

Waki' said: "We used to seek the help of good deeds when memorising hadith and seek the help of fasting when seeking knowledge."[87]

This principle is a very important principle, and it must be given due attention before and during the memorisation of the Quran.

As for the eye by which you memorise the Word of Allah, it should not look at that which Allah has prohibited it to look at. The ear with which you want to listen to the Word of Allah should not listen to that which has been forbidden by Allah to listen to. The heart which you hope will be a vessel for the Book of Allah, should be clean, pure and far away from turbidity and impurity.

SIXTEENTH PRINCIPLE – ORGANISED REVISION

Revising the memorised verses is as important as the memorisation itself, if not more. Memorisation can be easy for the *nafs* (the self) and can be attained with little motivation; whereas, revising that which has been memorised is difficult for the *nafs* and requires struggle and patience, especially in the early stages. (See Chapter 4 for a detailed discussion of different methods for revising the Quran.)

At this stage, it is sufficient to point its importance. Those who do not revise for a long period of time will forget what they have memorised and will need to exert new efforts to memorise it all over again.

Jaafar al-Sadiq said: "The hearts are [like] soil, knowledge is a plant, and revision is water. If water is not given to the soil, the plants will dry up."[88]

And may the mercy of Allah be upon the one who said: "Enrich knowledge with revision, for perseverance of knowledge is (in its) revision."

SEVENTEENTH PRINCIPLE - COMPREHENSIVE UNDERSTANDING

You should try to understand that which you are memorising as much as possible. But is this a general rule?

Small children and non-Arabs can memorise the Quran without understanding it. I have seen many who have memorised the entire Quran, yet they cannot speak a word of Arabic. Hence, this rule of understanding ceases to be a general rule.

What is meant by comprehension and understanding is that you should be able to grasp the meanings of the verses that you are memorising. If you come across a word that is confusing to you, refer back to a *tafsir* of the Quran as this will aid in your consolidation of your memorisation.

EIGHTEENTH PRINCIPLE - PERSONAL MOTIVATION IN MEMORISING THE QURAN

Educational experts define motivation as a concentration of inner power that drives an individual to achieve their goals. There is also another definition, which seems to be more precise: an internal physical and spiritual state which directs behaviour in a certain direction and enables the person to reach a specific goal.

If we were to ask ourselves: What are the motivations that make a Muslim memorise the Quran? There would be no doubt that the primary aim of a Muslim would be to attain the pleasure of Allah; the Quran is amongst the greatest mediums in achieving this aim. Allah has promised many rewards for the one who memorises the Quran in this life and in the next.

It is these motivations of attaining the pleasure and rewards of Allah and the virtues of the people of the Quran that instigate an internal state conducive to memorising the Quran.

It falls upon teachers to direct their students to these aims and instil in them a strong desire for memorisation.

NINTEENTH PRINCIPLE – DUA AND SEEKING THE HELP OF ALLAH

Many of the principles that I have mentioned so far are material in their application and as yet, I have not mentioned a spiritual principle. Hence, the last principle will be focussed on this latter and most important aspect.

Turning to Allah makes every hardship an ease. Depending upon Allah and seeking his help in times when memorisation becomes difficult for you is the best of all medicines. It once happened that a student was memorising *al-Shatibiyyah* (a long poem on the seven *qira'at*) and found one of the chapters very hard to memorise. He was left with nothing but to turn to Allah crying for His help at the time of dawn. It so happened that he was able to memorise the chapter very well.

It is narrated that Ibn Abbas was once in the company of the Prophet ﷺ when Ali came in and said: "O Messenger of Allah! You are dearer to me than my father and mother. I try to memorise the Quran but cannot do so as it vanishes from my memory." The Prophet ﷺ said: "Shall I tell you of a method that will benefit you as well as those to whom it is conveyed by you? You will then be able to retain whatever you learn." At the request of Ali, the Prophet ﷺ said: "When the night preceding Friday comes, wake up in its third portion if possible. This is the best part of the night as this is the time when angels descend, and prayers are especially granted at this hour. It was for this time that my brother Yaqub had been waiting when he said to his sons that he would, in the near future, pray to his Lord for forgiveness for them. If it is difficult to get up at this time, then you should get up in the middle part of the night. After reciting Surah al-Fatihah in each rakah (unit), Surah Yasin should be recited in the first rakah, Surah al-Dukhan in the second, Surah Alif Lam Mim Sajdah in the third, and Surah al-Mulk in the fourth. After completing salutations on the Prophet ﷺ, you should praise and glorify Almighty Allah abundantly, invoke peace and blessings upon all the prophets, seek forgiveness for all the believers who have passed away, and then recite the following dua: O Allah! Have mercy on me by enabling me to avoid sins as long as You keep me alive, and have mercy on me by enabling me to avoid falling into things with which I am not concerned, and allow me to look at only what pleases you. O Allah! The originator of the heaven and earth, master of majesty and benevolence and possessor of dignity which is incomprehensible. I beseech You, O Allah, O beneficent one, in the name of Your majesty and of the light of Your countenance to cause my heart to memorise Your book as you have taught me and grant me that I may be able to recite it in such a manner which will cause You to be pleased with me. O Allah! O Allah! The originator of the heaven and earth, master of majesty and benevolence and possessor of dignity which is incomprehensible. I beseech You O Allah, O beneficent one, in the name of Your majesty and of the light of Your countenance to illuminate my vision with the light of Your book, to set my tongue free with its [fluent] recital, to remove the grief of my heart with it, and to wash away the sins of my body with it. Certainly there is none except You to support me in attaining the truth, and none except You can give it to me. And there is no protection [against evil] and no power [to do good] except with the help of Allah, the most high, the most great."

The Prophet ﷺ further said to Ali: "Repeat this act for three, five or seven Fridays. If Allah wills, your dua (supplication) will certainly be granted. I swear by He who made me a prophet that the acceptance of a believer's dua will never be neglected." Ibn Abbas reports that hardly five or seven Fridays had passed when Ali came to the Prophet ﷺ and said: "Previously, I used to learn about four verses and wasn't able to retain them, but now, I learn about forty and I can remember them as clearly as if I had the

Quran open in front of me. Previously, when I heard a hadith and then repeated it, I could not retain it, but now, I hear a hadith, and when I narrate it to others, I do not miss a single word." The Prophet ﷺ then said: "A believer [you are definitely], by the Lord of the Kaaba, Father of al-Hasan."[89]

In your hands now are the nineteen principles. I pray to Allah that He gives you the ability to master them and use them to memorise the Quran.

As for the methodology and manners by which one memorises the Quran, they will be explained in detail in the following chapter.

Chapter 3

Practical Methods for Memorisation

In light of the principles that I have explained in the previous chapter, I will now move along to mentioning the most common methods for memorising the Quran. I have discussed every method separately, even if there are similarities between some of the methods. I believe that the variety of methods will open a way for everybody, at every level, at all ages and from all cultures to memorise the Quran. Perusing these methods will make the task of memorising the Quran easier, by the Help of Allah, on the condition that students abide by the aforementioned principles and conditions.

1 - THE IDEAL METHOD

From my own personal experience, this is the ideal method for memorising the Quran. Anyone above the age of ten may use it. The following guidelines should be followed with precision. Begin by choosing a good printed copy of the Quran, of any size that suits you, but do not ever replace this copy. It is preferable to choose the *mushaf*[90] that begins each page with the beginning of a verse and ends each page with the end of a verse. It is divided into thirty *juz*, with each *juz* consisting of twenty pages and each page having fifteen lines. Then prepare to sit and memorise the Quran using the following steps.

1. Prepare yourself mentally by making the intention to seek the pleasure of Allah. You should have an inner motiva-

tion of seeking the reward of Allah.

2. Be vigilant in your ablutions, and do not make concessions by using the fatwas (juristic dispensations) which say that there is no need for ablution when touching or reciting the Quran. Cleanliness and ritual purity should be part of our manners with the Glorious Quran.

3. Sit in a place in which you are at ease with yourself and at rest – mentally and spiritually. There is no better place for memorisation than the mosque.

4. It is preferable that the place in which you sit to memorise should not have any pictures, posters or anything distracting.

5. Sit facing the *qiblah* (the direction of prayer) with *khushu* (concentration), *sakeenah* (tranquillity) and *waqar* (dignity).

6. Begin your memorisation by warming up. Read a page from the Quran, either looking at it or not. This will prepare you spiritually for memorisation.

7. Do not get carried away with the beauty of your voice, for you may become engrossed in your recitation to the extent that you begin to visualise yourself as a famous *qari* (reciter), and this will waste a lot of time without your realising it.

8. After approximately ten to fifteen minutes of warming up and mental preparation, you will feel a strong desire and motivation to memorise the Quran; this is when you should begin to memorise.

9. Now begins a very important stage. You must concentrate extremely well on the verses and visualise that your eyes

are the lens of a camera intending to take a visual picture of the page.

10. Open your eyes and free your mind from other things. Read from the beginning of the page in a voice loud enough to be heard by others. Read the first verse three times or as many times as it takes you to memorise the verse. Then, with your eyes closed, visualise in your memory the exact location of the verse on the page and begin to read. If you are successful in reading it (from memory) without any mistakes, then do not feel successful. Rather, repeat the verse two, three or five times.

11. Then open your eyes for a second time, and read the verse from the *mushaf* to confirm that your memorisation was correct. If you are one-hundred per cent sure that you have memorised the verse correctly, still do not feel successful. Close your eyes and read it for a final time. By now, you will have engraved the verse in your memory, and it will not disappear, by the Will of Allah. Experiment with these steps with precision and you will begin to realise the soundness of this method.

12. During your memorisation and repetition, beware of casting glances at pictures or objects around you. Do not pay attention to the quality and type of furniture or bed that you are sitting on. Do not look out the window. If you do, you will begin to pay attention to the cars that are passing by. This happens to students when they are revising for their exams; one will stand by the window to breathe in fresh air and will begin to pay attention to the cars and their models, and before they have realised it, they have been distracted and have wasted time. Thus, you must pay utmost attention to your Quran and not get distracted by

other things. You have chosen to be amongst the people of the Quran.

13. Immediately after this, move on to the next verse. Repeat the steps you took to memorise the previous verse. If you find the verse too long, divide it into a few appropriate parts (in terms of stoppage and soundness in meaning). Repeat the verse until it becomes engraved in your mind.

14. Begin now to visually connect the verses (as I mentioned in the eighth principle in the previous chapter). This is done by concentrating on the ending of one verse and the beginning of the next. Connect the ending of the first verse with the beginning of the next by reading it without stopping. Repeat this practice at least five times.

If after reading the above steps, you feel motivated, then begin immediately. Record the date on which you begin memorising, and keep yourself accountable by telling someone you trust so that they can encourage you to keep memorising.

This ideal method for memorising the Quran can be summed up in the following steps: psychological preparation, warming up, concentration, repetition and connecting. The result will be solid memorisation.

2 - MEMORISATION BETWEEN TWO

I still remember what one of our teachers wrote on the board whilst I was studying shariah (Islamic law) at the Furqan Institute. He wrote, "Knowledge grows between two." For those who want to memorise using this method, they should abide by the following guidelines.

1. Choose a friend whom you have confidence in and who gives importance to that which you give importance to.

Agree to meet at a time that suits both of you. It is preferable that this time is after Fajr or between Maghrib and Isha and that this meeting is on a daily basis.

2. Agree to begin with a specific surah.

3. Open your *mushaf* and read the verse to be memorised as your friend listens and follows in their own *mushaf*. Then, listen to your friend's recitation while following in your *mushaf*. After this, recite the verse without the *mushaf* as your friend listens and vice versa.

4. Move on to the next verse in the same manner until the page is completed.

5. Then begin with the practice of connecting between the verses, as mentioned earlier, until you both feel that you have memorised the page completely and correctly.

6. Now begin to test yourselves. One of you should act as teacher and the other as student and then reverse the roles.

7. Each one of you should draw your companion's attention to their mistakes, so that they can take care not to make them again.

3- USING TIME WASTED IN CARS

Many of those who want to memorise the Quran have jobs and are very busy. They say, "I do not have time." Once I realised their sincerity and saw that many of them waste time during their commute to and from work, I decided to draw attention to this method.

1. Make a copy from your *mushaf* of the page you want to

memorise.

2. Place it in your car in a place that is in front of you but does not hinder you from driving.

3. Read the first verse and repeat it as you warm up the car in the morning.

4. When you begin to drive, repeat the verse, but this time without looking at it.

5. During your drive, look at the next verse whenever you stop at traffic lights. When you drive, repeat it to yourself without looking at it. And so on.

Take care of the pages that you photocopy, and do not discard them until they are worn out. It is advisable to cover the pages in a plastic cover. Once you have finished memorising a page, save it so that you may return to it a second time.

Do not look at the page whilst you are driving as this may cause an accident. Only look at the page when you stop the car to wait at traffic lights.

There are a number of scholars who have memorised using this method, but while using a bicycle or a riding animal. Shaykh Abdul Fattah Al Marsari, may the Mercy of Allah be upon him, was one such person. He used to memorise the *Tayyibah* (a text in the ten different recitations) on the back of a riding animal. I have also experimented with this method whilst I was in secondary school, and I memorised the *Alfiyyah* of Ibn Malik (a book on the grammar of the Arabic language) on a bicycle whilst going to the school. I found it very useful indeed.

4 - LISTENING

There are many ways in which one can benefit from the use of recordings; it will be sufficient to mention a few of them.

The First Technique

Choose a recording by a well-known reciter, such as al-Husary or al-Minshawi.

1. Listen to a surah from beginning to end.

2. Listen to it for a second time.

3. Listen to it for a third time, and this time, read along with the reciter.

4. When listening to it for the fourth time, read along with the reciter, but pause at the end of the first verse and repeat the verse on your own. If you make a mistake, then try it again. If you recite it correctly, then repeat it three times so that it is firmly rooted in your memory.

5. Move on to the second verse and repeat the technique by which you have memorised the first verse.

6. Do not forget to link the verses as discussed earlier.

This method is suitable to be used at home and in the car. However, if you wish to memorise at home, then pay attention to the following.

a. First of all, listen to the surah and follow the recitation in your *mushaf*.
b. Divide the surah into parts according to its meaning, making sure that each part does not exceed five verses.

c. Listen to the first part, then repeat it without looking at the *mushaf*. If you find the selected portion too long or difficult to memorise, then just learn half of it.

This method is very suitable for the blind. Many people have memorised the Quran using this method.

The Second Technique

This technique is similar to the first, except with the following differences. Listen to the recording whilst your head is on the pillow just before sleeping, when the lights are off and the night is calm and tranquil.

The Third Technique

1. Choose the surah you wish to memorise.

2. Listen to it on a regular basis for a week. Every time the recording finishes, begin it again and so forth.

3. At the end of the week, sit in the mosque between Maghrib and Isha and read the surah which you listened to throughout the week and try to memorise it.

4. You will be surprised to find that that you have memorised the surah very well and only required a minimal amount of concentration.

5. From the following day, begin with the next surah using the same technique. You will find yourself memorising very well, and it will not take much of your time.

This technique is suitable for those who have jobs. You should organise your own timetable to memorise a surah. I use the example of a week above, but this is merely an example. In most cases, it will take longer than a week to memorise a surah.

5 - RECORDING ONES'S RECITATION

People of different cultures and norms want to listen to beautiful voices and are moved to joy and delight when listening to them. But the only voice which will truly delight oneself is one's own voice. When you listen to your own recitation, you feel a sense of inner joy. Thus, one way to memorise the Quran is by using the following method.

1. Record yourself reciting the surah you intend to memorise, calmly and with *tajwid* (rules which are to be applied whilst reciting the Quran).

2. It is acceptable to divide the surah into several parts.

3. Listen to the recording of your recitation in the car, at home and in your garden, for this will help you to memorise at a fast pace and will motivate you to improve your recitation and memorisation.

4. Try to compare your recitation with the recitation of a well-known reciter. Try to notice the differences and mimic the reciter.

5. Try to repeat after your own recitation.

6. Determine exactly where you make mistakes in your recitation.

7. After you feel that you have memorised the surah very well, test yourself.

8. Test yourself by recording the surah you have memorised

without looking at the *mushaf* and then listening to it. Follow the recitation in the *mushaf* and identify any mistakes.

9. It is preferable to save your recordings.

6 - RECORDING A CHILD'S RECITATION

1. Choose a short surah that you want your child to memorise.

2. Record yourself reciting the first verse and your child repeating after you.

3. Ask your child to listen to the recording repeatedly and memorise the verses. Tell them that you will test them in the evening.

4. If you are not able to record your recitation daily, record a number of surahs for your child to memorise throughout the week. At the end of the week, test your child on every surah that they have memorised.

This method has been used and proved to be an excellent method. Our teacher, Shaykh al-Hafidh al-Jami al-Shaykh al-Sawid Lashin Abul-Fath, taught his son to memorise the Quran using this method, and he was able to memorise the complete Quran by the age of nine.

Children will be delighted to hear their own voice, and once they listen to the verses two or three times, they will be able to memorise them without any difficulty.

This method also has other benefits: children will begin to develop an independent personality and learn to depend on themselves while listening to the recordings on whichever device you choose. Children will begin to realise their own mistakes and begin to rectify them.

7 - WRITING

The ability to memorise varies from person to person. Some people have very sharp memories and are able to retain what they read even if they read it only once. Others have very weak memories and must listen to something repeatedly before they are able to memorise it.

The technique of writing in order to memorise is a very good technique, especially when compared to reading and listening.

This method can be applied in many ways.

1. Memorise five verses and concentrate on the lettering of the verses. After you have memorised them, try to write them down. Then compare what you have written with the *mushaf* and identify any mistakes.

2. The teacher writes down the verses that are to be memorised by the students in their textbooks and on the board. The students copy what their teacher has written. The teacher asks them to memorise from what they have written and then listens to their recitation. The students then write the verses but this time from memory.

One who memorises using this method will rarely forget.

8 -WRITING ON A BOARD

I present this method for those who want their children to memorise the Quran through a practical method. Many have experimented with this method and have benefited from it.

1. Buy a new white board with different coloured pens.

2. Hang the board in the child's room or in any other suitable place.

3. Write for them, in neat handwriting, the surah they will memorise. Write the words in black, put on the vowels in red and separate each verse with a green mark.

4. Ask your child to write the verses in their notebook without any mistakes.

5. Then ask them to memorise it throughout the day.

6. On the following day, test your child. Once you are confident that your child has memorised the surah, move on to another surah.

7. In order to encourage them, you can ask them to write on the board. They will try to copy your handwriting, and thus, their handwriting will improve.

8. Parents may worry about the time that will be required for such an endeavour. But once you begin this method, it will not take more than fifteen minutes to write the surah on the board and approximately thirty minutes to listen to your child and correct their memorisation. If we are honest with ourselves, we will admit that many hours are wasted daily on television and movies. We cannot waste our own time and our children's time in these pursuits and then complain that our children are weak in their studies or find it difficult to memorise the Quran. Devoting time to the education of our children will result in honour in this life and reward in the Hereafter.

9 - WRITING ON A BOARD WITH A TEACHER

This method is very similar to the previous method because it is based on writing, but I am including it as a separate method because of its importance and significance. The technique to be used is as follows.

1. In the first stage, the teacher writes the verses to be memorised by the student on the board or slate.

2. The teacher then asks the student to read, letter by letter, and then tells them to memorise.

3. The student then wipes the verses off of the board and rewrites them from memory.

4. The teacher corrects the writing as well as the memorisation of the verses.

5. When the teacher is confident that the student has memorised the verses, they move on to the next verse, and so on.

6. Whatever is memorised using this technique cannot be forgotten.

I was once with some Mauritanians who had memorised using this technique, and I noticed that they had memorised the Quran as completely as each one of us have memorised our names. This method still exists and continues to be used in Mauritania, Sudan and other Muslim countries.

10 – COMPETITIONS AND REWARDS

There are many ways in which a Quran memorisation competition can be used as a method to memorise the Quran.

Friends

1. Agree with your friends at school, college, or work that each one of you will memorise a selected surah within three days.

2. After three days, get together in a mosque or in another suitable place.

3. Each person should stand and recite the amount they memorised.

4. The one with the least amount of mistakes will get a star next to their name. This should be done for a month in order to see who has the most stars alongside their name.

5. The one who obtains the most stars should be rewarded with a book, pen, toy, cash, or other prize.

Teachers with Students
Teachers should tell students about the benefits of the Quran and the stories of those who have memorised it and encourage them to memorise as well.

Mosques and Islamic Centres
These institutions should give out prizes to those who have memorised the Quran.

Parents with Children
Parents should reward their children for each surah they memorise. These rewards may come in the form of presents, but parents should make it clear that they are receiving these gifts because of the Quran they memorised.

Spouses with Each Other
Spouses should compete with each other to see which one of them can memorise the most in a month and so on. They should give each other gifts as a reward, regardless of who the winner is.

11 - FROM THE END OF THE PAGE

1. Open the *mushaf* to the page which you intend to memorise.

2. Instead of memorising from the top of the page, go to the last verse of the page and memorise it.

3. Then move on to the verse which is before it and memorise it. Continue doing this until your reach the top of the page.

Islamic law prohibits this method because of the reversal in the arrangement of the verses, but if one memorises each verse on its own and does not link to the next verse, perhaps the prohibition will be lifted.

This method is regarded as very useful to master the memorised material. Many people memorise the beginnings of pages and surahs in a solid manner because their determination is strong at the beginning, but by the time they reach the end, their determination is weakened, and they become lazy in their memorisation. This is why we see many who complain that they do not know the ends of the surahs as well as they know the beginnings.

I have also heard of many blind people reading Surah Ibrahim using this method and memorising it very well. I do not recommend this method. However, during the course of memorisation, one may sometimes become bored. Rather than stopping the memorisation, it is better to change the method of memorisation to relieve oneself of boredom.

12 - LINE BY LINE

1. Open the *mushaf* to the page you intend to memorise.

2. Use a blank piece of paper to cover the page, showing only the first line.

3. Read the first line until you memorise it.

4. Move the paper so that you can read the second line. Memorise it.

5. Connect the first line with the second line in order to consolidate the memorisation.

6. Gradually move the paper from line to line until the end of the page and until you have memorised each line. You will, by the Will of Allah, have achieved results with which you will be pleased.

7. Use the same method for the second page, and so on.

A brother informed me that his friend memorised the Quran using this technique.

13 –USING VIDEO

There is no doubt that video is a useful educational tool when used properly. One can make use of video to memorise the Quran in a variety of ways. Here is one.

1. A reciter can record the whole Quran. Students will not need to view the video more than three times and will have memorised it, by the Will of Allah.

2. The recitation should be at a medium pace – not very fast nor very slow.

3. The video should also consist of the written text of the Quran: as each verse is recited, it should also appear written on the screen.

4. There is no doubt that this method requires an institution for its implementation. Preparing the videos will require

professionals with specialist knowledge.

There are also other techniques.

1. A teacher can be recorded reciting a verse, and then a student can repeat after them. This recording is better than the recording of the teacher alone because students watching will hear the verse twice, in two different voices.

2. Record your own recitation or the recitation of a child and begin the memorisation as outlined previously.

14 - USING A COMPUTER

This method is similar to the previous method and can be done in many ways.

Memorisation through Typing

1. Display the page you want to memorise on the monitor and begin to memorise it.

2. Then open a word processor and type what you have memorised. Then compare what you typed with a *mushaf.*

Memorisation through Listening

Use a programme that allows you to listen to the recitation of the verses by a reader of your choice. This method is similar to the use of audio recordings, but a computer program will typically allow you more options.

15 - LINKING VERSES WITH SPECIFIC TIMES

Time-linking can be used to link your memorisation with times that you will not forget. For example, on the night of Jumu'ah, memorise Surah al-Kahf. On the night of Laylah al-Qadr, memorise another surah. This process of linking the memorisation with a specific time will help consolidate your memorisation.

One of our scholars – Shaykh Mahmud Abdul Dayim Al-Misri (90 years old) – told us that he memorised the text of *al-Sulam* under the rays of the moonlight, without a lamp, while his relatives were engrossed in a discussion on agricultural seasons.

Often in the Quran, Allah links verses with a certain time, thus highlighting the importance of time-linking. Allah says:

> And recite the Quran in the early dawn. Verily the recitation of the Quran in the early dawn is ever witnessed.

Allah says in another place:

> Verily We have sent it (this Quran) down in the night of Qadr.

16 - LINKING MEMORISATION WITH SIGNIFICANT EVENTS

Many events occur in the life of a human being. Some we forget, and others we retain even into our old age. If you are able to link your memorisation with significant events, then this will help you consolidate your memorisation. Every time you recall the event, you recall the verses memorised. There are many examples of this in the *sirah*.

1. In the cave of Hira, when the Messenger of Allah received revelation for the first time, the angel Jibril ordered him to read. He replied, "I am not a reader." Jibril asked him three times, and the Messenger of Allah gave the same reply each time. Then the Prophet ﷺ read the first five verses of Surah al-Alaq. These verses became engraved in his memory as this was an unusual event.

2. The spoils of war and the prisoners at the Battle of Badr

was linked with Surah al-Anfal.

3. Many battles had specific parts of the Quran revealed about them. Some examples are Badr, Uhud and Hunayn, among others.

4. The event of the slander (*ifk*) of Aisha ؓ was the reason for the revelation of some verses.

Here are some other examples that are not limited to a certain time period.

1. Many who are held in detention or are incarcerated emerge having memorised the Quran.

2. Many who fall ill and spend a long period in bed or in the hospital find this period helpful to memorising the Quran. I know someone who fell ill and could not leave his house. He memorised the Quran in four months.

17 - LINKING THE VERSES WITH SENSATIONS

During your memorisation, your intellect should be ready and free from distractions. Try to link your memorisation with your sensations and with things that inspire your feelings (for example, the sky, earth, mountains, other creatures, etc.) When you read "and it is He who has subjected the sea (for you)", try to visualise the sea in your mind and link the verse with that mind's eye view.

When you read "Do they not see the birds held in the midst of the sky?" look up at the sky, try to find a bird and link the verse with it.

When you read "And if they were to see a piece of the heaven falling down, they would say: 'Clouds gathered in heaps' ", look up to the clouds in the sky.

When you read "Yes, we are able to put together in perfect

order the tips of his fingers," look at your own fingers.

Linking the verses with your sensations will help you consolidate your memorisation and will also aid you in your revision. If you forget a word, you may be able to remember the sensation you linked it with and recall the word.

18 - UNDERSTANDING

This is a method which depends on the explanation and meanings of words, the clarification of ambiguous words and the reasons for the revelation of the verses. This method is appropriate for adults and not children.

1. Get a *mushaf* and a basic *tafsir* (exegesis) of the words of the Quran.

2. Select the verses to be memorised.

3. Read the verses concentrating on words that are strange or unfamiliar to you.

4. Open the *tafsir* and find the meanings of the words that were unfamiliar to you. Try to find out the reason for the revelation of the verses if possible. What I mean by "the meanings of the words" is the partial meaning of the part you are reading and want to memorise. As for the surah itself, it has a complete and linked meaning based on a focal point. (Amongst those who have focused on this issue and explained it is Dr Abdullah Darraz ﵀ in *al-Naba al-Adhim*.)

5. You will by now have formulated a clear and complete picture of the verses.

6. Begin memorising, while concentrating on the meanings

of the verses.

7. If you are able to memorise the verses and understand them, there is nothing for you to do except practice that which you have memorised and understood. This was the method of the Companions. As Abdullah ibn Umar said: "We used to take ten verses – memorise them, understand them and then practice them."

8. Move on to the next verse and follow the same steps.

19 - THE BLIND

Sight is a blessing from Allah, but we hardly realise its value. A scholar once said to me: "If you want to understand the value of your sight, put a bandage over your eyes for one hour. You will realise the value of what Allah has given you. Thank Allah for this blessing and let not your eyes see things that do not please Allah."

To those to whom Allah has not given sight, He has given deep insight and a higher level of intellect. They are able to memorise faster than others. The methods that should be used by the blind vary from person to person. I will suffice with the following.

1. The blind person, whatever their age may be, should have a teacher who has memorised the Quran. This is a very important principle of memorisation in general but especially for the blind. It does not matter if the teacher is visually impaired or not, although a blind teacher might be more aware of the needs of the blind student.

2. If it is not possible to find a teacher, it is acceptable to rely on a friend who recites correctly. The friend should be someone suitable to help them memorise the Quran.

3. If a friend cannot be found, it is possible to depend on

audio recordings of the Quran.

4. A quiet place should be chosen, far away from any noise or disturbances.

5. The teacher or friend should read the verses to be memorised one by one and then ask the student to repeat the verse two or three times until they memorise it.

6. The teacher or friend should then move on to the next verse and repeat the same technique until the whole page has been memorised.

7. The number of verses to be memorised depends on the ability of the blind student.

8. The most important point is that the student must revise daily that which has been memorised. If they cannot recall a word, they may move on to the next word, but they should later ask their teacher or friend about it.

The role that audio recordings of the Quran play in the memorisation of the blind should not be underestimated, especially when a teacher or friend cannot be found.

I have met many blind *huffadh* (memorisers), and, in most cases, their memorisation is better than others, and they have told me that they memorised using the method outlined above.

20 - ATTENDING CIRCLES

The circles for memorising the Quran have increased in the mosques in a number of Muslim countries. This increase is evident in Saudi Arabia, where there are more than a thousand circles. This is due to the efforts exerted in the service of the Quran. It began with an Indian man named Shaykh Yusuf. He wanted to build a Quranic school in India and needed *huffadh* to teach the Quran. He thought to bring *huffadh* from Mecca – the land of Quran and the place of revelation. When he reached Mecca, he found that the people of the Quran were few in number, and thus, he decided to start his work in Mecca itself. He started the first circle of memorisation in Masjid al-Haram and from there many circles were established.

In most mosques, the following method is used.

1. The teacher announces the opening of a circle to memorise the Quran in the mosque. A certain number of people of all ages gather.

2. The teacher begins to teach the short surahs. The students repeat after the teacher.

3. The teacher assigns a certain amount that the students should memorise in order to recite the following day.

4. Once students have memorised their portion, they read it to the teacher and move on to the next portion.

5. That is why we observe that students who attend one designated circle are stronger in their memorisation than others.

6. It has been observed that students who study in circles often move their bodies during memorisation. This movement of the body is beneficial in many ways. Primarily, it helps in giving energy to the heart. If you were to compare two students – one who does not move their body during memorisation and one who does – you would find that the second student has memorised more than the first. I do not ask students to move back and forth whilst mem-

orising, but, if during the course of their memorisation, they feel the desire to move, then there is no harm in that.

7. The role of the teachers in these circles is to listen; the effort must be put forth by the students.

8. The capabilities of students differ widely. Some are able to memorise the whole Quran whilst others leave the circle without completing their memorisation. The profitable one is the one who continues.

9. The teacher should keep a daily record of what each student has memorised.

10. Those who are good at memorising should be rewarded and given prizes in the circles or in an annual ceremony that takes place at the mosque.

11. An annual ceremony should be organized to reward the students who have memorised the entire Quran and have become *huffadh* (memorisers). Parents, teachers and scholars should be present at this ceremony.

21 - ROTATION

This is a method that I saw in Sudan, and it is not as strange as it may sound. I describe this method to my readers for curiosity's sake, but I do not recommend its use. Many still memorise using this method and find it extremely useful. It is as follows.

1. The teacher of the circle will recite to the student the quarter that each one of them has reached. The teacher will correct their recitation, pronunciation, and writing (on their slates).

2. The teacher sits in the middle of the circle and supervises. Students approach one-by-one and recite to the teacher, who corrects their recitation.

3. This continues for approximately two hours, during which time each student will have memorised their portion. Students normally sit on mats, which is very tiring and can lead to laziness and a lack of concentration. Thus, the teacher orders the students to begin the second stage.

4. This stage is known as "rotation". The students line up in a circle and walk slowly around the teacher, who remains in the middle and supervises.

5. During their rotation, students revise the portion they memorised while sitting.

6. They are permitted to raise their voices a little, and they are active and motivated.

7. After an hour of rotation, they sit. They then take a second turn reciting to the teacher. They read with high spirits.

There are many benefits to this method. The rotation aids blood circulation and activates the bones and the heart after long periods of sitting. For children, who will naturally get bored after sitting still for two hours, this rotation helps change the mood of the lesson to excitement and activity.

22 – THE UZBEKISTANI METHOD

This method is prevalent in some of the Muslim states that became independent after the collapse of the Soviet Union: Kyrgyzstan, Kazakhstan, Dagestan, and, especially, Uzbekistan. I mention it here for the sake of knowledge and information. The method is as follows:

1. Students begin by correcting their recitation using the first page of the Quran with their teacher.

2. The teacher orders students to repeat the first page three hundred times while looking at the *mushaf.*

3. Once students have repeated the first page three hundred times, they read to the teacher from memory. In this manner, students memorise the next page and so on, until they have completed the Quran.

4. When students have completed the memorisation of the Quran, the teacher orders the student to read the Quran one hundred and fifty times looking at the *mushaf.*

5. When this recitation is completed, students are then named *hafidh* (memoriser) or *qari* (reciter).

It seems that reciting the Quran so many times makes the verses roll off the tongue. This is a phenomenon that we can see with surahs that we recite often (such as Surah al-Kahf) – they often become semi-memorised. This is due to the repetition.

23 - THE TURKISH METHOD

The role that Turkey plays in the field of the Glorious Quran should not be underestimated, and it seems appropriate to mention the Turkish method of memorisation.

1. Students practice reading the Quran while looking at the *mushaf* for a long period of time. They are also taught the alphabet, until their recitation is perfectly correct. This may take up to a year. They then move on to the second

stage – the stage of memorisation.

2. During memorisation, they use a *mushaf* in which the Quran is divided into thirty parts (*juz*); each part contains twenty pages, and each page consists of fifteen lines.

3. Students begin with the last page of the first *juz*. The following day, they move on to the last page of the second *juz*. They continue until they have completed the last page of each of the thirty *juz*. This will have taken one month.

4. In the beginning of the next month, students memorise the second to last page of the first *juz*, and the following day, they memorise the second to last page of the second *juz*, and so on.

5. This is continued until students have memorised the entire Quran in reverse order. Every time a student memorises a page, they read it to the teacher, along with all the previously memorised pages. Thus, the memorisation becomes reinforced, like engraving onto a slate.

Scholars have differed over the permissibility of this method – some praise it whilst others criticise it. When I asked some of the notable scholars of Istanbul about this method, they said: "This is what we have inherited from our scholars." All of them regard it as the best method to memorise the Quran to the extent that some Turks cannot imagine another way to memorise the Quran.

In reality, if one ponders this method, it has many benefits, especially for those who don't know Arabic. Its fruits are apparent if students continue this method until they have memorised the entire Quran. These students' memorisation will be strong, and they will even know the page numbers and *juz* numbers of everything they've memorised.

However, one of its drawbacks is that if a student does not continue with this method until the end and stops for any reason, they will have only memorised sections from here and there without any connection. If such a student were asked to recite a surah, they would not be able to do so. It would also be difficult for them to resume memorisation.

This method cannot be implemented partially. It must be implemented fully. It will also require at least two full years for it to bear any fruit.

FOODS WHICH HELP IN MEMORISATION

As a supplementary benefit, I want to mention the views of the people of knowledge regarding foods which aid in memorisation.

Al-Zuhri said: "Eat honey; it is good for memorisation." Honey is a cure for people as the Quran says: "There comes forth from their bellies, a drink of varying colour wherein is healing for people."

In your tea, use honey instead of sugar. You will find it to be delicious. Others advise that instead of drinking tea, drink herbal mint tea with black seed oil and a spoonful of natural honey. You will have a clear memory throughout the day and will feel active.

Chapter 4

Revision and Consolidation

If Allah honours you by enabling you to memorise the Quran, then this is a blessing from Allah and a trust that you must carry with you and not neglect by lack of revision. This stage is probably even more important than the first stage of memorisation. The Messenger of Allah said: "Make this Quran a contract. By the One in Whom my soul is in His Hands, it slips away faster than a camel slips away from its cord."

It has been narrated that Jaafar al-Sadiq said: "The hearts are soil, knowledge is the plantation and revision its water. If the water is cut off from its soil, the plantation will become dry."

Al-Khatib al-Baghdadi said: "The student should guard that which they have memorised, revise all of it at specific intervals and not be careless of it. If some of the scholars taught someone anything, after a certain period of time, they would ask them about it. If they remembered, then the scholars would teach them; if not, they would ask them to return and memorise the Quran."

There are many ways to revise, and they vary from person to person. Some of these methods will be outlined here. Revision is generally done individually or with someone else.

INDIVIDUAL REVISION

Those who have memorised the Quran should be able to depend on themselves and formulate a daily timetable that suits them. The timetable can be formulated in many ways.

First Way

You can read five *juz* (parts) a day and thus complete a whole revision of the Quran in six days. It is said that "the one who devotes themselves to the reading of five will not forget."

Second Way

Divide the Quran into seven sections. (This was most common amongst the pious predecessors.) Ibn Jama'ah said: "The reading of the Quran in seven days is a good practice. It has been mentioned in the hadith, and Ahmad ibn Hanbal used to practise it."

According to this method, the revision of the Quran is divided throughout the seven days of the week, so that every Friday a complete revision of the Quran has been made. The timetable will thus look as follows:

Day	Section	From	To
Saturday	1	Surah al-Baqarah	Surah al-Maidah
Sunday	2	Surah al-Maidah	Surah al-Yunus
Monday	3	Surah al-Yunus	Surah al-Isra
Tuesday	4	Surah al-Isra	Surah al-Shuara
Wednesday	5	Surah al-Shuara	Surah al-Saffat
Thursday	6	Surah al-Saffat	Surah Qaf
Friday	7	Surah Qaf	Surah al-Nas

Once a complete revision has been made, you should begin with the next revision. This method is common in Mauritania, and it is one of the reasons the memorisation of Mauritanians is so strong.

I would advise those who have just finished their memorisation of the Quran to revise the Quran for at least six months using this method. Their memorisation will surely be consolidated.

Third Way

Revise three *juz* daily and complete the Quran in ten days. Thus, every month you will complete the Quran three times.

Fourth Way

Choose three *juz* for each week and repeat them throughout the week. For example, begin on Saturday and end on Friday. You will have read the three *juz* seven times. The following week, begin with another three *juz*. Thus, you will have completed the whole Quran in ten weeks, and will have read it seven times.

Fifth Way

Revise the Quran twice. In the first revision, revise two *juz* every day and repeat them throughout the week. In the second week, move on to another two *juz*. During the second revision, read a new *juz* every day. Thus, the average revision will be three juz daily. In a month, you will have completed one complete revision of the Quran and consolidated eight *juz*.

I propose this method for those who have memorised the Quran but have not been regularly revising it and have forgotten some parts of the Quran.

Sixth Way

Revise one *juz* daily, thus completing the Quran once every month. It is not befitting for the person who has memorised the Quran to do less than this. Some call this way "the standard of the lazy".

Seventh Way

Make use of *qiyam al-layl* (night prayers). It has been found to be very useful. Shaykh Abdul Fattah al-Musafi ﵀ used to pray eleven rakahs (units) of *witr* (an odd-numbered final prayer) daily and read three *juz*. Our Shaykh, Fath Muhammad Pani Patti (shaykh of the Pakistani recitors) used to read ten *juz* everyday in *salah al-tahajjud* (night prayers).

Make use of *tarawih* during Ramadan. It is an opportunity for the memorisers. They should lead the *tarawih*, reading one *juz* daily. This will require you to revise thoroughly before leading the prayers, not less than five times.

Make use of the *sunnah* and *nafl* prayers. Most of us recite short surahs in our prayers. However, if we recite half a page in every rakah of *sunnah* every day, we will be able to revise approximately half a *juz* a day.

Eighth Way

Make use of recordings and listen to them frequently at home, in the car and before sleeping.

Ninth Way

Re-memorise the Quran, especially the ends of the surahs. The lapse of time can cause one to forget the Quran to the point that it is as if it had never been memorised. This is a very useful method and has been used by many. If you forget a surah or any part of the Quran, re-memorise it as though you are memorising it for the first time.

REVISION WITH SOMEONE ELSE

It is preferable that you revise with your teacher. This type of revision can also take many forms.

First Way

Revise what you just memorised. This method is for beginners in memorisation. In it, the student recites a certain portion of their memorised surahs every day. The teacher should not let the student proceed to a new portion until the old portions have been memorised and revised thoroughly. The memorisation should not contain any mistakes.

Second Way

Revise with a friend the page you memorised the day before. Thus, every day you will memorise a page and revise a page.

Third Way

Revise as the Messenger of Allah revised with the angel Jibril. We know from the hadith related by Imam Bukhari that Jibril used to come to the Messenger of Allah once every Ramadan and check the recitation and memorisation of the Messenger of Allah. In the Ramadan preceding his death, Jibril came twice.

To benefit from this method, abide by the following steps.

1. Agree with a friend to revise the Quran on a monthly, weekly or daily basis. The latter option is preferable.

2. Begin with the revision of Surah al-Baqarah, for example. One of you should read the first quarter of the first *hizb* (half of a *juz*) and the other should follow along in the *mushaf*.

3. Then, reverse roles so that the one who was listening now reads and the one who was reading now follows along in the *mushaf*.

4. At the end of the sitting, one of you should ask the other a question concerning the verses you have revised.

5. This method is known as *mudarasah* and is one of the best methods of revision.

Chapter 5

Advice and Recommendations

SPECIFICALLY – FOR THOSE WHO HAVE COMPLETED THEIR MEMORISATION

After Allah has honoured you with the memorisation of the Quran, abide by the following guidelines. I have already mentioned some of these points, but I repeat them here because of their importance.

6. Search for a teacher who has a high *sanad* (chain of transmission) reaching all the way to the Messenger of Allah. Do not settle for your local school or mosque. The one who has memorised the Quran but has not been checked by a teacher who has a *sanad* and an *ijazah* may have a deficient memorisation that is not free from mistakes.

7. After you have recited the entire Quran to your teacher and have received an *ijazah*, there is no harm in searching for another teacher who has a stronger *sanad*. Reading to different teachers will allow you to acquire different talents from different people.

8. Memorise a *matn* (a condensed poem that outlines the rules of a science) on *tajwid*. (You should memorise at least *al-Jazariyyah*, and if you feel you can memorise more, then memorise *al-Shatibiyyah*.)

9. It is incumbent upon you to regularly revise the Quran in an organized manner, as I have outlined previously.

10. Make use of *qiyam al-layl* (night prayers) in order to recite the Quran. It is indeed extremely beneficial.

11. Make use of the *tarawih* prayers in Ramadan.

12. Many of those who have memorised the Quran complain of not knowing the endings of surahs as well as they know the beginnings. Memorise them again and you will feel the enjoyment of the memorisation that you had left for a long time.

13. During your revision, try to interact with the meanings. At every revision, try also to increase your knowledge of the verses.

14. Always carry a copy of the Quran in your pocket and never separate from it regardless of where you go. The Quran is your best friend, and you should take care of and pay attention to it. Also, do not change your copy of the Quran.

15. When you are reading to your teacher, have a pen and a notebook with you. Record the useful things you learn from your teacher. Many of us have forgotten many useful sayings that we heard from our teachers. May Allah be pleased with the one who said, "Knowledge is hunting, and writing is its shackles. Tie that which you have hunted with a strong rope, for it is stupidity to hunt a bear and then let it go."

16. Keep a record of your sessions with your teacher and the places and circles in which you read the Quran. Record the

names of other scholars who listened to your recitation as well as those present on the day you completed your recitation of the Quran. If you are able to, ask your teacher to sign your book – this book will in later years become very valuable and will hold memories. I still have my book to this day. I have recorded the place and time in which I read every verse and the scholars who listened to my recitation and their comments. This is not an innovation but has been practiced by many of our pious predecessors.

GENERALLY – FOR THE PEOPLE OF THE QURAN, STUDENTS OF KNOWLEDGE AND THE YOUTH

1. Have sincerity of intention in every step you take. Sincerity is the secret of *tawfiq* (success) and the opening from Allah. The hadith is well-known.

   > Actions are but by intentions. For every one is that which they intended. The one who migrated for the sake of Allah and His Messenger, then truly their migration was for Allah and His Messenger. And the one who migrates for the world or to get married, their migration is for that which they migrated to.

2. Beware of committing sins, of all types and forms, but especially those committed with the eye and ear. Think of your heart as a basin; if your pour ink into water, its purity will be destroyed.

3. Choose friends who believe in and fear Allah, so that they will help you in your memorisation of the Quran. They will encourage you and remind you in times of laziness or hardship. Search for the friendship of those who possess

strong determination and seriousness and exert their utmost efforts to attend the circles of knowledge.

4. Beware of watching TV and following films and soaps. They will wipe the Quran from your heart and plant in its place the love of passions. After a time, your heart will become hard and will not be affected by the recitation of the Quran. You will not be able to obtain *khushu* (concentration) in your prayers.

5. Beware of reading filthy magazines with obscene pictures, as they corrupt the character and are destructive for the youth. Do not even read them out of curiosity, for that is not your business. Your business is the revision of that which you have forgotten from the Book of Allah and reading other books of knowledge.

6. Think deeply about matters and refrain from superficiality.

7. Use a daily exercise program to keep your body fit and in shape. But do not become so attached to it that you spend the majority of your time training. An hour a day is sufficient.

8. Stay away from games such as backgammon, cards, and chess. You are among the people of the Quran and are above such triviality and insipidity.

9. Guard every minute of your time. Be careful how you spend it, in what and with who. The time of the believer is more valuable than gold, for time is life with which to buy Paradise.

10. Seek the advice of the people of knowledge in that which

you read.

11. Spend your youth memorising the Quran. Once you have memorised it, turn your attention to Islamic texts, such as *al-Jazariyyah*, *al-Bayquniyyah*, *al-Rahbiyyah* and *Alfiyyah ibn Malik*.

12. Beware of disobeying your parents. Treat them with kindness, for their prayers for you will be accepted by Allah.

13. Refrain from spending time in your room on your own doing nothing useful. Organise your time so that you do not complain of having too much spare time. Spare time kills youth.

14. If you are alone in your room, refrain from committing bad deeds: remember that you are really not alone. Allah sees you, and the angels around you record each and every movement you make. Remember that your hands will testify against you if you use them in a way that does not please Allah. Allah says:

    > This Day, We shall seal up their mouths, and their hands will speak to Us, and their eyes will bear witness to what they used to earn.

15. Beware of sitting in the circles of the people who are drowning in this worldly life. These gatherings will harden the heart.

16. Assess your heart and intention while in company. Do not fall into pride, hypocrisy or showing off.

17. Ask yourself every night before you sleep: What have I

done for the service of Islam today? What will I do for it tomorrow?

18. Keep a journal of the important events that take place in your daily life. Record your thoughts and plans.

19. Read on a regular basis. Let not a day pass without reading at least fifty pages from a book.

20. Do not be miserly but be abundant in the remembrance of Allah, sending salutations on the Messenger of Allah and seeking forgiveness. There is no better way to end your day than by remembering Allah.

May Allah guide us to His guidance.

Conclusion

Finally, after reading this book, you will realize the important results that are now in front of you.

1. This book was written in response to a question posed by many: "How can I memorise the Quran?"

2. Those who want to memorise the Quran will now see wide horizons and different practical methods of memorisation based on the experience of the specialists in the field.

3. This book has laid out the principles and theoretical rules of memorisation, and it has also taken into account the practical methods of memorisation, thus balancing the two aspects – theory and practice.

4. This book has not neglected the aspect of revision, for its importance is no less than that of memorisation itself. I have outlined at least ten methods by which a student can revise.

5. This book has also concentrated on the importance of learning and memorising the Quran by receiving it from the scholars and the importance of obtaining an *ijazah* (a certificate showing the chain of readers back to the Prophet [s]).

6. I have also ended this book with some advice and recommendations that are important for those who have memorised the Quran and for students of knowledge.

I would like to thank all those respected teachers and scholars who have read this book, have written endorsements and have provided feedback, which I paid great attention to.

I ask Allah to accept that I have done this work solely for His Pleasure.

Yahya Gawthani
29 Shawwal, 1414
10 April, 1994

Endnotes

1 al-Buruj 85:21–22
2 al-Zukhruf 43:4
3 al-Jinn 72:26–27
4 Tafsir ibn Kathir, 4/462
5 al-Jinn 72:8
6 al-Jinn 72:9
7 al-Qiyamah 75:16–19
8 Bukhari, Tafsir
9 al-Furqan 25:32
10 al-Qasas 28:51
11 al-Maidah 5:67
12 al-Najm 53:3–4
13 al-Baqarah 2:151
14 al-Hijr 15:9
15 al-Qamar 54:17
16 Tafsir al-Qurtubi, Surah al-Qamar
17 al-Ankabut 29:49
18 Bukhari, Maghazi, 53
19 Bukhari, Jana'iz, 73
20 Bukhari, Nikah, 50
21 Tirmidhi, 2914
22 al-Jami li Akhlaq al-Rawi Adab al-Sami, al-Khatib al-Baghdadi, 1/42
23 Bukhari, 9/839; Muslim, 891
24 Muslim, 789; Muwatta, 1/202
25 Abu Dawud, 461; Tirmidhi, 2917

26 Musnad of Imam Ahmad, 5/327
27 Taha 20:99–100
28 Taha 20:124–126
29 Tafsir al-Qurtubi, Surah Taha
30 al-Shura 42:30
31 Fadhailul Quran, 112
32 al-Isra 17:79
33 Diwan Imam Shafi'i, 81
34 Sha'b al-Iman, 4/359
35 al-Zumar 39:11
36 Muslim, 6/47
37 al-Jami li Akhlaq al-Rawi wa Adab al-Sami, al-Khatib al-Baghdadi, 2/213
38 Bukhari, Beginning of Revelation, 1
39 Musnad al-Firdaus, narrated by Daylami, 2735
40 al-Sha'b, narrated by Baihaqi, 4/507
41 al-Tarikh al-Kabir; Bukhari, 3/94
42 al-Fiqh wal-Mutafaqqih, 2/103
43 al-Jami fi al-Hath ala Hifdh al-Ilm, 177
44 al-Jami fi al-Hath ala Hifdh al-Ilm, 177
45 al-Fiqh wal-Mutafaqqih, 2/103
46 Bukhari, Tawhid, 44
47 al-Darmi, Fada'il al-Quran, 24
48 al-Jami fi al-Hath ala Hifdh al-Ilm, 174
49 This *mushaf* (printed edition) ends every page at the end of a verse, and each *juz* (part) has twenty pages; this helps one to memorise the Quran systematically.
50 al-Jami fi al-Hath ala Hifdh al-Ilm, 190
51 Tabaqat al-Shafi'iyyah, al-Subki, 8/213; Tabaqat al-Mufassirin, al-Dawudi, 1/313
52 al-Jami fi al-Hath ala Hifdh al-Ilm, 254
53 al-Jami fi al-Hath ala Hifdh al-Ilm, 254
54 al-Hath ala Talab al-Ilm wal-Ijtihad, Abu Hilal al-Askari, 32
55 al-Hath ala Talab al-Ilm wal-Ijtihad, Abu Hilal al-Askari, 36

56 al-Hath ala Talab al-Ilm wal-Ijtihad, Abu Hilal al-Askari, 40
57 al-Hath ala Hifdh al-Ilm wa Dhikr Kibar al-Huffadh, Ibn al-Jawzi, 225
58 al-Fiqh wal-Mutafaqqih, 2/100
59 al-Fiqh wal-Mutafaqqih, 2/100; al-Jami li Akhlaq al-Rawi wa Adab al-Sami, 2/129
60 al-Furqan 25:32
61 Hud 11:67
62 al-Araf 7:78
63 al-Baqarah 2:61
64 Ali Imran 3:21
65 Ali Imran 3:112
66 al-Risalah al-Mufassalah li Ahwal al-Mutaallimeen wal-Mutakallimeen, from Adab al-Mutaallim fi Fikr al-Tarbawiyyah al-Islami, Ahmad Muhammad Falatah, 97
67 Ruh al-Tarbiyyah wal-Taleem, Muhammad Atiyyah al-Arashi, 165, from Adab al-Mutaallim fi Fikr al-Tarbawiyyah al-Islami, 97
68 Jami Bayan al-Ilm wa Fada'ilihi, Ibn Abdul Barr, 1/77
69 Taleem al-Mutaallim wa Turuq Taallum, 41
70 Taleem al-Mutaallim wa Turuq Taallum, 43
71 al-Shura 42:38
72 Muhadarat al-Udaba wa Muhawarat al-Shu'ara al-Bulagha, al-Raghib al-Isfahani, 1/28
73 Tadhkir al-Sami wal-Mutakallim fi Adab al-Alim wal-Mutaallim, Ibn Jama'ah, 85
74 Ibid., 85
75 Ibid., 85
76 al-Jami fi al-Hath ala Hifdh al-Ilm, 177
77 al-Jami fi al-Hath ala Hifdh al-Ilm, 177
78 Juz fihi Akhbar li Hifdh al-Quran, Ibn Asakir, 226
79 al-Maidah 5:13
80 Juz fihi Akhbar li Hifdh al-Quran, Ibn Asakir, 227
81 Juz fihi Akhbar li Hifdh al-Quran, Ibn Asakir, 228
82 Juz fihi Akhbar li Hifdh al-Quran, Ibn Asakir, 228

83 al-Saff 61:3

84 Ihya Uloom al-Din, Imam al-Ghazali, 1/65

85 Ayyuha al-Walad, Imam al-Ghazali, 99

86 al-Najm 53:39

87 Hifdh al-Quran, Ibn Asakir, 229

88 al-Jami li Akhlaq al-Rawi wa Adab al-Sami, al-Khatib al-Baghdadi, 2/334

89 al-Hakim, 1/316; Tirmidhi, 10/18

90 *Mushaf* is a word used to refer to a printed copy of the entire Quran.